SCIENCE EXPLORER JUNIOR

JUNIOR SCIENTISTS
Experiment with Plants

by Susan H. Gray

CHERRY LAKE PUBLISHING · ANN ARBOR, MICHIGAN

NOTE TO PARENTS AND TEACHERS: Please review the instructions for these experiments before your children do them. Be sure to help them with any experiments you do not think they can safely conduct on their own.

NOTE TO KIDS: Be sure to ask an adult for help with these experiments. Always put your safety first!

CHERRY LAKE Publishing

Published in the United States of America by Cherry Lake Publishing
Ann Arbor, Michigan
www.cherrylakepublishing.com

Content Editor: Robert Wolffe, EdD, Professor of Teacher Education, Bradley University, Peoria, Illinois
Reading Adviser: Cecilia Minden-Cupp, PhD, Literacy Consultant

Design and Illustration: The Design Lab

Photo Credits: Page 15, ©Katrina Leigh/Shutterstock, Inc.; page 17, ©BestPhoto1/Shutterstock, Inc.; page 22, ©Lucian Coman/Shutterstock, Inc.; page 23, ©Tilborg Jean-Pierre/Shutterstock, Inc.; page 27, ©John Boud/Alamy.

Library of Congress Cataloging-in-Publication Data
Gray, Susan Heinrichs.
  Junior scientists. Experiment with plants / by Susan H. Gray.
      p. cm.—(Science explorer junior)
  Includes bibliographical references and index.
  ISBN-13: 978-1-60279-839-7 (lib. bdg.)
  ISBN-10: 1-60279-839-7 (lib. bdg.)
  1. Plants—Experiments—Juvenile literature. I. Title. II. Title:
Experiment with plants. III. Series.
  QK52.6.G73 2010
  580.78—dc22   2009048822

Portions of the text have previously appeared in *Super Cool Science Experiments: Plants* published by Cherry Lake Publishing.

Cherry Lake Publishing would like to acknowledge the work of The Partnership for 21st Century Skills. Please visit *www.21stcenturyskills.org* for more information.

Printed in the United States of America
Corporate Graphics Inc.
July 2010
CLFA07

TABLE OF CONTENTS

Let's Experiment!

Experiments
are fun!

Have you ever done a science **experiment**? They
can be a lot of fun! You can use experiments to
learn about almost anything.

Scientists observe the world around them.

This book will help you learn how to think like a scientist. Scientists have a special way of learning new things. Some people call it the Scientific Method. This is how it often works:

- Scientists notice things. They **observe** the world around them. They ask questions about things they see, hear, taste, touch, or smell. They come up with problems they would like to solve.

A scientist makes a guess called a hypothesis.

- They gather information. They use what they already know to guess the answers to their questions. This kind of guess is called a **hypothesis**.

- Then they test their ideas. They perform experiments or build models. They watch and write down what happens. They learn from each new test.

Scientists record what happens during their experiments.

- They think about what they learned and reach a **conclusion**. This means they come up with an answer to their question. Sometimes they conclude that they need to do more experiments!

When a scientist figures out the answer to her question, she has reached a conclusion.

Conclusion: Plants need sun and water to grow.

There are probably many kinds of plants in your neighborhood.

We will use the scientific method to learn more about plants. Plants are an important part of our world. Grass, trees, and flowers are all plants. Plants are living things. Have you ever wondered how they eat and drink? How do they grow? We can find the answers to these questions and more by doing experiments. Each experiment will teach us something. Are you ready to think like a scientist?

Roots and Shoots

A plant has both roots and a stem.

First, we'll gather some information. What do you already know about plants? You probably know that they grow from seeds. You probably also know that plants grow both above and below ground.

A stem grows up from the ground. Roots grow down below.

The root and stem both grow from the seed. But which one starts growing first? We can answer this question with a simple experiment. First, we'll need a hypothesis. Here are some possible hypotheses:

1. Roots start to grow before stems do.
2. Stems start to grow before roots do.
3. Roots and stems start to grow at the same time.

Let's get started!

Write down your hypothesis.

Roots and stems start to grow at the same time.

Here's what you'll need:

- A clear plastic cup with 3 holes punched into the bottom. Ask an adult for help punching the holes with scissors or another sharp tool.
- A saucer or tray to put under the cup
- 4 beans. You can use dried beans such as pinto or lima. You can find these at the grocery store.
- A warm spot, such as a sunny windowsill
- Potting soil
- Water
- A marker

Find a sunny spot.

Potting Soil

Plant the beans and water them.

Instructions:

1. Fill the cup with potting soil.
2. Plant your beans in the cup. They should be about 1 inch (2.5 centimeters) deep. Place the beans close to the sides of the cup so you can see them.
3. Place the cup on a saucer or tray.
4. Water the seeds, and set the cup in a warm spot.

5. Check the seeds every day. Keep the soil moist but not soaking wet.

6. Look at the plants every day until the shoots have grown about 1 inch (2.5 cm) above the soil. Write down your observations each day. Pay attention to which part of the plant grows first.

Conclusion:

Was your hypothesis correct? You should have noticed that the roots grew before the stem. Plants need roots to get water and other things they need to grow from the soil. Roots also keep the plant stuck in the ground.

Do you see the roots in this picture?

Light or Dark

Plants need sunlight, but how much do they need?

All living things need energy to live and grow. Plants need energy from sunlight. How much sunlight do plants really need? We can use an experiment to find out. First, we'll start with a hypothesis. Here are some choices:

1. Bean plants grow best when they have sunlight all day long.
2. Bean plants grow best with just a little sunlight each day.
3. Beans plants grow best with no sunlight.

Now you can set up an experiment to test the hypothesis.

How much sunlight do plants need?

Here's what you'll need:

- A marker
- 3 cups filled with potting soil. Each cup should have 3 young bean plants growing inside it. Grow just one type of bean. The tallest plants should be no more than 2 inches (5.1 cm) tall.
- 3 saucers or trays for the cups to sit in
- A warm, sunny spot such as a windowsill
- 2 empty boxes or coffee cans that are big enough to cover the cups
- Water

Collect your supplies.

Cover the "0" and "2" hour cups.

Instructions:

1. Use the marker to label the cups "0 hours," "2 hours," and "All day."
2. Place the cups on the saucers or trays, and put them in a sunny spot.
3. Use the boxes or coffee cans to cover the "0 hours" and "2 hours" cups.

4. Observe the plants for the next 10 days. Be sure to keep the soil moist during the experiment.

5. Keep the "0 hour" cup covered except when you water it.

6. Uncover the "2 hour" cup for 2 hours each day.

7. Leave the "All day" cup uncovered the whole time.

8. Write down what you see happening to the plants each day. What color are the leaves?

Conclusion:

Which plant looks healthiest after 10 days? Which one looks the sickest? How can you tell? Look at the leaves. Are they brown and wilted or green and full? Plants with brown, wilted leaves are not healthy. Was your hypothesis correct? You should have found that the plant that got the most sunlight was the healthiest.

Which plants grew the most? Record what you find.

How Do Plants Drink?

Plants need water to grow.

In the first two experiments, you had to water the plants. The plants used the water to grow. How do the plants drink the water? We know the plants get the water from the soil. How does the water get from the soil to the leaves? Let's do an experiment to find out. Here is a hypothesis we can test: Water travels to a plant's leaves through tubes in the stem and other parts of the plant.

How does water get to the tops of tall plants?

Here's what you'll need:

- A stalk of celery with leaves attached
- A small kitchen knife
- A glass jar
- Water
- Red or blue food coloring
- A warm, sunny spot

Collect your supplies.

Ask an adult to help you cut the end of the celery stalk.

Instructions:

1. Have an adult cut the stalk of celery near the bottom.
2. Place the celery in the glass jar with the cut end down.
3. Pour about 1 inch (2.5 cm) of water into the jar.
4. Add 6 drops of food coloring.

Record what happens every 15 minutes for the next 4 hours.

5. Place the jar in a warm, sunny spot.

6. Check on the stalk every 15 minutes for 4 hours.

7. After 4 hours, gently rinse the stalk and its leaves.

Conclusion:

How do the leaves look? You should notice that they have turned the color of the food coloring. Remove the stalk of celery from the jar. Have an adult cut it in half. Look at where it was cut. Do you see the tubes? Did they also change color? What does that tell us about how leaves get their water? Was our hypothesis correct?

Can you see the tubes that carried the water through the celery?

What other questions do you have about plants?

Okay, scientists! Now you know many things about plants. You learned that roots are the first part of a plant to grow. You also learned that plants grow best when they get enough sunlight. Finally, you learned that leaves get water through tubes in the stem and other parts of the plant. You learned these things by thinking like a scientist.

Do you have some more questions about plants? Maybe you are wondering if plants grow best when it is warm or cool outside. You might wonder if plants grow bigger when they get more water. Why not use your scientific thinking skills to answer these questions? You're a Junior Scientist now, so give it a try!

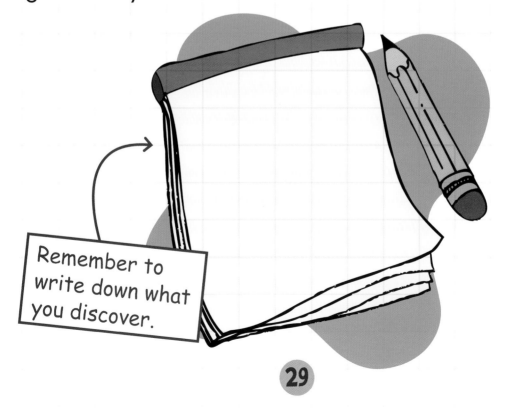

Remember to write down what you discover.

GLOSSARY

conclude (kuhn-KLOOD) to make a final decision based on what you know

conclusion (kuhn-KLOO-zhuhn) a final decision, thought, or opinion

experiment (ecks-PARE-uh-ment) a scientific way to test a guess about something

hypothesis (hy-POTH-uh-sihss) a guess about what will happen in an experiment

observe (ob-ZURV) to see something or notice things by using the other senses

FOR MORE INFORMATION

BOOKS

Cook, Trevor. *Experiments with Plants and Other Living Things.* New York: PowerKids Press, 2009.

Hoffman, Mary Ann. *Plant Experiments: What Affects Plant Growth?* New York: PowerKids Press, 2009.

WEB SITES

National Geographic Kids—Make a Cool Terrarium!
kids.nationalgeographic.com/Activities/Crafts/Miniature-garden
Find out how to turn a jar or fishbowl into a miniature garden.

National Junior Horticultural Association—Experiments & Fun Activities
www.njha.org/experiments.html
Discover some more activities involving plants.

INDEX

ABOUT THE AUTHOR

Susan H. Gray has a master's degree in zoology. She has written more than 100 science and reference books for children and especially loves writing about biology. Susan also likes to garden and play the piano. She lives in Cabot, Arkansas, with her husband, Michael, and many pets.